18.00

The Arctic Habitat

Molly Aloian and Bobbie Kalman

🌱 Crabtree Publishing Company

www.crabtreebooks.com

Created by Bobbie Kalman

Dedicated by Michael Vincent
To Samm, and all her "kids".

Editor-in-Chief
Bobbie Kalman

Writing team
Molly Aloian
Bobbie Kalman

Substantive editor
Kathryn Smithyman

Editors
Michael Hodge
Kelley MacAulay
Rebecca Sjonger

Design
Margaret Amy Salter
Samantha Crabtree
   (cover and series logo)

Production coordinator
Heather Fitzpatrick

Photo research
Crystal Foxton

Special thanks to
Jack Pickett and Karen Van Atte

Illustrations
Barbara Bedell: page 15
Barb Hinterhoeller: page 26
Katherine Kantor: pages 22, 27, 30, 32 (walrus)
Bonna Rouse: pages 20, 32 (bird and flower)
Margaret Amy Salter: page 32 (burrow)

Photographs
iStockphoto.com: Gordon Laurens: page 21 (bottom)
Photo Researchers, Inc.: W. K. Fletcher: pages 14, 27; Tom McHugh: page 22
Visuals Unlimited: Charles George: page 28
Other images by Corbis, Corel, Creatas, Digital Stock, Digital Vision, Eyewire, and Photodisc

Library and Archives Canada Cataloguing in Publication

Aloian, Molly
   The Arctic habitat / Molly Aloian & Bobbie Kalman.
(Introducing habitats)
Includes index.
ISBN-13: 978-0-7787-2953-2 (bound)
ISBN-10: 0-7787-2953-2 (bound)
ISBN-13: 978-0-7787-2981-5 (pbk.)
ISBN-10: 0-7787-2981-8 (pbk.)
   1. Ecology--Arctic regions--Juvenile literature.
I. Kalman, Bobbie, date. II. Title. III. Series.

QH84.1.A46 2006   j577.0911'3   C2006-904087-7

Library of Congress Cataloging-in-Publication Data

Aloian, Molly.
   The Arctic habitat / Molly Aloian & Bobbie Kalman.
      p. cm. -- (Introducing habitats)
Includes index.
ISBN-13: 978-0-7787-2953-2 (rlb)
ISBN-10: 0-7787-2953-2 (rlb)
ISBN-13: 978-0-7787-2981-5 (pb)
ISBN-10: 0-7787-2981-8 (pb)
   1. Ecology--Arctic regions--Juvenile literature.   I. Kalman, Bobbie.
II. Title.
QH84.1.A46 2007
577.0911'3--dc22
                                                      2006018061

Crabtree Publishing Company

www.crabtreebooks.com   1-800-387-7650

Published in Canada
Crabtree Publishing
616 Welland Ave.
St. Catharines, ON
L2M 5V6

Published in the United States
Crabtree Publishing
PMB16A
350 Fifth Ave., Suite 3308
New York, NY 10118

Published in the United Kingdom
Crabtree Publishing
White Cross Mills
High Town, Lancaster
LA1 4XS

Published in Australia
Crabtree Publishing
386 Mt. Alexander Rd.
Ascot Vale (Melbourne)
VIC 3032

Contents

What is a habitat?

A **habitat** is a place in nature. Plants live in habitats. Animals live in habitats. Some animals make homes in habitats.

Living and non-living things

There are **living things** in habitats. Plants and animals are living things. There are also **non-living things** in habitats. Rocks, water, and dirt are non-living things.

Everything they need

Plants and animals need water,
air, and food. Water, air, and food
help keep plants and animals alive.
Plants and animals have everything
they need in their habitats. This
mink found a fish to eat.

Homes in their habitats

Some animals have homes in their habitats. This mother arctic fox has a home for her and her babies. Their home is among some rocks.

The Arctic

The **Arctic** is a habitat.
It is at the top of Earth.
The Arctic is very cold.
There is a lot of snow
and ice in the Arctic.
Polar bears live in
the Arctic.

The Arctic Ocean

There is a very cold ocean in the Arctic. It is called the **Arctic Ocean**. Ice floats on the Arctic Ocean. Some animals rest on the ice. This harp seal is resting on ice.

Arctic weather

The weather is very cold in the Arctic. There are long, cold winters. Winter lasts for most of the year. In winter, there are **blizzards**. Blizzards are snowstorms. Blizzards have strong winds.

Short summers

In the Arctic, summers are short. The weather is not very warm. The snow melts in only some places. Some plants grow in these places. Animals eat the plants. Some animals, such as this grizzly bear, go to the Arctic in summer to eat plants.

Arctic plants

In summer, plants grow in the Arctic.
The plants grow close to the ground
because strong, cold winds blow.
Growing close to the ground helps
protect arctic plants from these winds.

Colorful flowers

Some arctic plants have colorful flowers. This plant is a dwarf willow herb. It has bright pink flowers. It grows only during summer.

Plants make food

Living things need food to stay
alive. Plants make their own food.
They make food from sunlight,
air, and water. Making food from
sunlight, air, and water is
called **photosynthesis**.

Making food

A plant gets sunlight through its leaves. It also gets air through its leaves. A plant gets water through its roots. A plant uses sunlight, air, and water to make food.

Leaves take in air.

Leaves take in sunlight.

Roots take in water from soil.

15

Arctic animals

These animals live in the Arctic. The Arctic is their habitat. The animals find food in their habitat. They also find homes.

snowy owl

polar bears

arctic tern

arctic fox

seal

caribou

arctic squirrel

17

Staying warm

Arctic animals need to stay warm. Many arctic animals have thick fur. The fur covers their bodies. This musk ox has thick fur. Fur helps keep the musk ox warm.

Warm blubber

Many arctic animals have **blubber** under their skin. Blubber is thick layers of fat. Blubber helps keep the animals warm. This walrus has blubber under its skin.

Finding food

Animals must search for food in the Arctic. Some animals eat only plants. Animals that eat plants are called **herbivores**. Lemmings are herbivores. They eat grass.

Eating animals

Some arctic animals are **carnivores**. Carnivores are animals that eat other animals. This arctic fox is a carnivore. It eats birds, fish, and arctic hares.

Omnivores

Some arctic animals are **omnivores**. They eat plants. They also eat other animals. This ptarmigan is an omnivore. It eats plants, seeds, and insects.

Getting energy

sun

All living things need **energy**. They need energy to grow and to move. Energy comes from the sun. Plants get energy from the sun. Animals get energy by eating food. A lemming is a herbivore. It gets energy by eating grass.

grass

lemming

Eating for energy

Carnivores get energy by eating other animals. An arctic fox is a carnivore. It gets energy by eating lemmings.

Staying safe

Some arctic animals hunt other animals. The animals that are hunted need to stay safe. Animals stay safe in different ways. Some move quickly. They can run away from animals that hunt them. This snowshoe hare can run quickly.

Hiding out

Some arctic animals stay safe because other animals cannot see them. This baby seal has white fur on its body. Its fur blends in with the white snow around it. The baby seal is safe because it is hard to see.

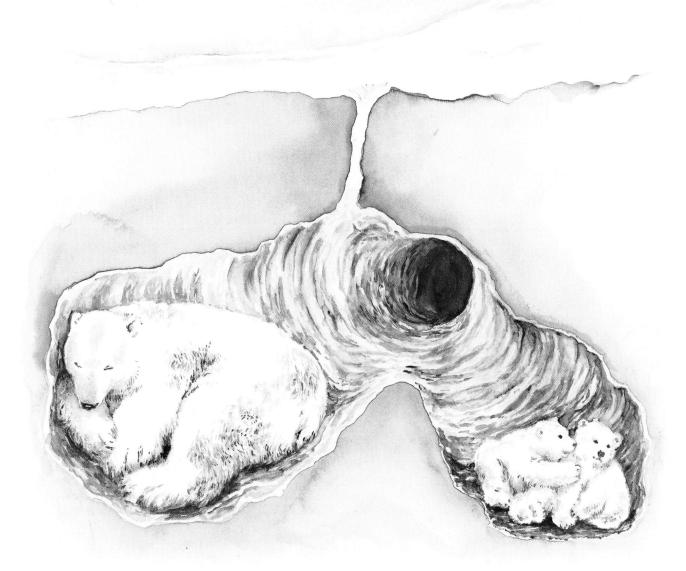

Arctic homes

Some arctic animals make homes.
They keep warm inside their homes.
This mother polar bear has made
a home for her babies. The home is
called a **den**. The den is in the snow.

Making nests

Many birds make homes called **nests**. Snowy owls, arctic terns, and other birds make nests. In summer, these birds lay eggs in their nests. Baby birds hatch from the eggs. The baby birds live in the nests.

Going to sleep

Winter in the Arctic is very cold. It is too cold for some animals. These animals go to sleep. They sleep all winter. They sleep in warm dens. This arctic squirrel sleeps through winter.

The animals wake up!

The sleeping animals wake up at the beginning of summer. They come out of their dens. They are hungry. They look for food to eat.

Leaving the Arctic

Some arctic animals do not sleep through winter. They leave the Arctic before winter begins. They move to warmer places where they can find food. These arctic terns are flying to a warmer place.

Caribou groups

Caribou also leave the Arctic in winter. They leave in big groups. The groups of caribou walk to warmer places. Caribou sometimes swim across rivers during their trip.

Words to know and Index

animals
pages 4, 5, 6, 9, 11, 16-17, 18, 19, 20, 21, 22, 23, 24, 25, 26, 28, 29, 30

Arctic
pages 8, 9, 10, 11, 12, 13, 16, 18, 19, 20, 21, 24, 25, 26, 28, 30, 31

energy
pages 22, 23

food
pages 6, 14, 15, 16, 20, 22, 29, 30

habitats
pages 4, 5, 6, 7, 8, 16

homes
pages 7, 16, 26, 27

plants
pages 4, 5, 6, 11, 12-13, 14, 15, 20, 21, 22

sleep
pages 28, 29, 30

Other index words
carnivores 21, 23
herbivores 20, 22
living things 5, 14, 22
non-living things 5
omnivores 21
photosynthesis 14
water 5, 6, 14, 15

32

Printed in the U.S.A.